God's Word Is Our Prescription For Healing
You Better Take Your Medicine!

Annette Madlock Gatison

Unless otherwise indicated, all Scripture quotations are taken from the King James Version of the Bible.

Scripture taken from THE MESSAGE (MSG) Copyright ©1993, 1994, 1995, 1996, 2000, 2001, 2002 by Eugene H. Peterson. Used by permission of Nav Press Publishing Group.

Healing Prayer based on a prayer written by Germaine Copeland for Prayers that Avail Much for Women Special Gift Addition, Harrison House Publishers, 1997 for Word Ministries, Inc. Used by permission.

Unless otherwise indicated all cancer related definitions are from the National Cancer Institute Dictionary of Cancer Terms at http://www.cancer.gov/dictionary.

Disclaimer

The content in this book *God's Word is Our Prescription for Healing: You Better Take Your Medicine!* is provided for informational purposes only. The content is not intended to replace professional medical advice. Always seek the advice of your physician, or other qualified health care provider working with your physician, with questions you may have regarding any medical condition. The content of *God's Word is Our Prescription for Healing: You Better Take Your Medicine!* is not intended to be relied on for medical diagnosis or treatment. Never disregard medical advice, or delay seeking treatment, because of information that you have read in any book.

DEDICATION

To my dear friend Lisa M.T. who was of strong and virtuous character with a courageous, patient, loving, and kind, spirit.

CONTENTS

ACKNOWLEDGMENTS

Thank you to my church families in Minnesota, Maryland, Connecticut, and the District of Columbia each one has taught me something different about worship, God's Word, and the love of Jesus.

Thank you to everyone who reviewed this manuscript.

Forward

Why me?

Ever since the words "you have breast cancer" were uttered, there were things I needed to know that went beyond disease specific medical facts and statistics. My mind was reeling with thoughts of, "How can I handle this? What am I supposed to do? Why cancer? Why breast cancer?" I cried out loudly with anguish "Oh Lord, Why me?"

First things first, let me take this opportunity to give you a little background about myself, and why I have chosen to write concerning the healing word of God and the healing ministry of Jesus. I was diagnosed with two varieties of aggressive breast cancer. I found the first type in my right breast in early 2003 during a self-breast exam. I must admit I do not know what compelled me to do a self-breast exam in 2003; I can only say a little voice in my head told me to do one, as it was not something I did on a regular basis. In 2004, I completed the standard course of treatment for that time which for me included lumpectomy, chemotherapy, and radiation. Followed by five years of daily ingestion of an oral drug called Tamoxifen[1].

The second type of breast cancer was found in my left breast in the fall of 2009 during a routine mammogram. Again, I was given the standard course of treatment for that time period of lumpectomy, chemotherapy, and radiation along with Herceptin[2] completing this process in 2011. The summer of 2012 culminated in a bilateral mastectomy with breast reconstruction. The decision to have this body and mind altering surgery came after much prayer and contemplation. I spent many days and nights talking to God, pondering, thinking, and evaluating what it means to live with a breast cancer (BRCA) genetic mutation[3]. This was all very agonizing and of course this was not the end of it.

The treatment for cancer comes with a litany of side effects, those that you experience while undergoing the actual treatment such as nausea and vomiting, skin discolorations, various allergic reactions, chemo induced alopecia[4], and weight gain or weight loss to name the most common. In addition to these there are also the lingering and more long-term side effects that are disclosed and discussed to anyone undergoing the type of cancer treatment that I endured such as: neuropathy[5], chemo brain (cognitive issues with memory), lymphedema, arthritis, vision, and a litany of other residual health effects. My health was failing me, my body turned against me, and the mental stress was also taking its toll. This experience might be similar to other breast cancer survivor's stories, but none are ever exactly the same. Breast cancer, its treatment and aftermath are as unique as the individual and one size does not fit all. The additional health challenges I experienced just added to the multitude of questions I had for God. Always wondering why me, and what did I do to deserve this curse called cancer. The religious teaching I experienced up until this point indicated that it was God's will. I just could not accept this as an answer. My prayers could not continue to be God heal me if it is Your will and if it is Your will for me to be sick, let that be Your will. Unacceptable.

To help me answer those questions a dear friend did two things. First, she invited me to attend Living Word Christian Center's Healing School (Brooklyn Park, MN), which at that time was a weekly support group and Bible study for those suffering from many afflictions. I was curious to see if the Healing School ministry at Living Word was still in existence and was saddened to see however that it appeared to no longer exist. I searched the church website and did not see it listed among their ministries, Bible studies, or outreaches. I can only speculate as to why based on my own experience. If individuals were showing up expecting an instant healing and Benny Hinn[6] miracle crusade moments they were disappointed.

Secondly, she provided me with a healing devotional by St. Mark Brazee, one that I continue to use. I do believe that miracles are possible but are not always "charismatic" and instantaneous in their manifestations some times they are soft and subtle. It also takes a strong and consistent faith for the healing miracles of Jesus to manifest in this day and age; so much evil, negativity, and bad news can keep us from our healing because it all leaves too much room for doubt.

PREFACE

Now faith is the substance of things hoped for, the evidence of things not seen.

Hebrews 11:1

It is important for you to know that I believe God's healing power is available and channeled through the medical professions. Continue to work along with your medical professionals to bring about a sense of total well-being. I also believe that prayer and faith practices add to the sense of wholeness and healing. My goal is to address wellness of the mind, body and spirit, lift you up, and provide you with some tools to assist you in your fight for your life and soul.

Grasping on to the concept of faith healing is not an easy thing to do for some. I will speak for myself coming from a conservative religious background it was never even discussed. And the laying on of hands are you kidding. Faith healing and the concept of the laying on of hands have an enduring stigma attached to it that is not helped by some televangelists and other questionable faith healers. It has taken me years to finally get the understanding and lose the fear associated with fully believing in the promises of God when it comes to health and healing by faith and touch. Changes had to be made in how I believed and what I believed.

It has all been very complicated and filled with anxious moments with many more details than I will disclose here. The fact is that I have lived through cancer and a near death experience and this absolutely has everything to do with my belief in faith healing and the miracles that Jesus performed in His ministry. It was truly only after I faced up to that near death experience was I able to move to the next level of faith in my journey with God. During these experiences my faith has been stretched and my understanding of spiritual warfare[7] (Ephesians 6:12) has also grown exponentially. How else might one explain the unexplainable?

This is not medical advice. I am not a physician or medical professional. I am merely an individual who has experienced the healing power of faith in and through Jesus.

Inclusive Language

God's Word is Our Prescription for Healing: You Better Take Your Medicine! is written using traditional theological masculine pronouns for God, Jesus, and the Holy Spirit. The masculine gender identification of God in the Bible is not unanimous. I believe that God is neither male nor female.

God is said to give birth in the book of Job and portrays Himself as a mother in Isaiah, and there are many more references to female characteristics of God. Nonetheless many feminist and womanist theologians from various faith traditions argue for the consistent use of inclusive language. Again, I chose to use the traditional masculine pronouns for ease of understanding and consistency.

---

[1] A drug used to treat certain types of breast cancer in women and men. It is also used to prevent breast cancer in women who have had ductal carcinoma in situ (abnormal cells in the ducts of the breast) and in women who are at a high risk of developing breast cancer. Tamoxifen is also being studied in the treatment of other types of cancer. It blocks the effects of the hormone estrogen in the breast. Tamoxifen is a type of antiestrogen. Also called tamoxifen citrate.
[2] A drug used to treat breast cancer that is HER2-positive (expresses the human epidermal growth factor receptor 2). It is also used with other drugs to treat HER2-positive stomach cancer that has not already been treated and has spread to other parts of the body. It is being studied in the treatment of other types of cancer. Herceptin binds to HER2 on the surface of HER2-positive cancer cells, and may kill them. It is a type of monoclonal antibody. Also called trastuzumab.
[3] According to the National Cancer Institute *BRCA1* and *BRCA2* are human genes

that produce tumor suppressor proteins. These proteins help repair damaged DNA and, therefore, play a role in ensuring the stability of the cell's genetic material. When either of these genes is mutated, or altered, such that its protein product is not made or does not function correctly, DNA damage may not be repaired properly. As a result, cells are more likely to develop additional genetic alterations that can lead to cancer.

Specific inherited mutations in *BRCA1* and *BRCA2* increase the risk of female breast and ovarian cancers, and they have been associated with increased risks of several additional types of cancer. Together, *BRCA1* and *BRCA2* mutations account for about 20 to 25 percent of hereditary breast cancers and about 5 to 10 percent of all breast cancers. In addition, mutations in *BRCA1* and *BRCA2* account for around 15 percent of ovarian cancers overall. Breast cancers associated with *BRCA1* and *BRCA2* mutations tend to develop at younger ages than sporadic breast cancers.

A harmful *BRCA1* or *BRCA2* mutation can be inherited from a person's mother or father. Each child of a parent who carries a mutation in one of these genes has a 50 percent chance of inheriting the mutation. The effects of mutations in *BRCA1* and *BRCA2* are seen even when a person's second copy of the gene is normal.
[4] The lack or loss of hair from areas of the body where hair is usually found. Alopecia can be a side effect of some cancer treatments.
[5] A nerve problem that causes pain, numbness, tingling, swelling, or muscle weakness in different parts of the body. It usually begins in the hands or feet and gets worse over time. Neuropathy may be caused by cancer or cancer treatment, such as chemotherapy. It may also be caused by physical injury, infection, toxic substances, or conditions such as diabetes, kidney failure, or malnutrition. Also called peripheral neuropathy.
[6] A Televangelist with a healing ministry that performs instantaneous healings on audience members through the laying on of hands.
[7] Spiritual warfare is war with sin and sinful personalities. While all human beings are victims of spiritual warfare, its primary combatants are God and His angels and children, who are opposed by Satan and his demons. It is warfare between the kingdom of God and the Kingdom of the Devil. Murphy (1992).

CHAPTER ONE
HEALING PRESCRIPTION

"I am the Lord that healeth thee."

Exodus 15:26

*"My son, attend to my words; incline thine ear unto
my sayings. Let them not depart from thine eyes; keep
them in the midst of thine heart. For they are life unto
those that find them, and health to all their flesh."*

Proverbs 4:20-22

God's principles of divine healing are not always
explicitly stated, they are interwoven throughout the
Scriptures as an integral part of His redemptive plan.
According to Romans 5:12 the appearance of sickness and
death into the world is attributable to the original sin of
Adam. Sickness is not God's will or plan for our life as
Jesus redeemed us with his death on the cross. Knowing
this is the beginning of holding on to the plan God has for
our health and well-being. We must know what God says.
We must hear God's Word about healing, we must read
God's Word about healing, and keep His Word about
healing in our heart at all times.

*And not only so, but we also joy in God through our
Lord Jesus Christ, by whom we have now received the
atonement. Wherefore, as by one man sin entered into
the world, and death by sin; and so death passed upon
all men, for that all have sinned: (For until the law sin*

1

was in the world: but sin is not imputed when there is no law. Nevertheless death reigned from Adam to Moses, even over them that had not sinned after the similitude of Adam's transgression, who is the figure of him that was to come. But not as the offence, so also is the free gift. For if through the offence of one many be dead, much more the grace of God, and the gift by grace, which is by one man, Jesus Christ, hath abounded unto many.

Romans 5:11-15

In the midst of our illness we must remember the character and attributes of the God who created us. Our God is:

- Spirit – He dwells within us;
- Holy – Never been touched by sin;
- Eternal – Has always existed;
- Infinite – Without limits except when He has limited Himself by His Word;
- Omnipresent - Everywhere at once;
- Omniscient – All knowing;
- Omnipotent – All mighty;
- Truthful – Never lies;
- Just – Actions are one hundred percent fair;
- Righteous – One hundred percent good;
- Life – He is life;
- Unchangeable – James 1:17 says "Every good gift and every perfect gift is from above, and comes

down from the Father of lights, with whom there is no variation or shadow of turning";

- Sovereign – Absolute supreme ruler;
- Love – He is the most loving personality
- Faithful – God is always faithful – Romans 3:3 and 4;
- Merciful – St. Luke 6:36 says God is merciful. The amplified version of the Bible uses the following adjectives to describe God's mercifulness: sympathetic, tender, responsive, and compassionate;
- Provident – Watches over and cares for His creation, us.

It is erroneous to think that God would send sickness into someone's life to teach him or her a lesson or to get his or her attention. I have heard this idea preached and taught, and it is wrong. It is totally wrong. Our God wants us healed. He sent His Son to redeem us from the curse of the law. Many Christians, myself included, have unfairly attributed the sickness and disease to acts of God and not the evil one from whom they truly come. We should be standing against the enemy, the one who comes to steal, kill, and destroy, we should be standing against the works of the devil through the redemptive power of Jesus and be healed. How do we do this? We have to be able to recognize who is doing what in our lives so we can rightly apply God's healing Word.

*The thief cometh not, but for to **steal**, and to **kill**, and to **destroy**: I*

am come that they might have life, and that they might have it more
abundantly.

St. John 10:10

Remember that God is no respecter of persons (Acts
10:34), and He never changes (Malachi 3:6). So what He
said yesterday, He is saying to today. God's Word on
healing is for us today. God never changes His mind (St.
Matthew 4:4, St. Matthew 8:16, St. John 1:1,14; St. John
15:7, Psalms102:20, and Isaiah 55:11). Our enemy the devil
attempts to distract us from God's promises and twists the
truth. We must guard our hearts and minds against these
attacks on our mind, body, and soul.

A common assumption when people talk about
healing is that the conversation becomes narrowly focused
on issues of the body. I use the words disease and illness to
signify conditions that require prayer and faith that move
one towards restoration of wholeness of the mind, body,
and spirit. Again, one should remember that our physical
bodies are not the only part of us. We are composed of
body, mind, and spirit. The Bible gives scriptural reference
to every body part and every type of disease encountered
by the human body.

CHAPTER TWO
THE RETURN OF SPIRITUALITY TO THE ALLOPATHIC HEALING ARTS

The medical establishment has turned to various alternative medicine traditions – that include prayer and meditation to work in conjunction with medicine. Recent studies have shown that patients who have some sort of spiritual practice such as prayer (Christian/Protestant traditions), meditation (new age, Eastern, and other religious practices) have better health outcomes. In my research, I found many articles by medical professionals that referred to the importance of spirituality and the correlation to positive health outcomes. I will briefly discuss two here.

The purpose of the following articles: *Observations on prayer as a viable treatment intervention: A brief review for healthcare providers* by Kutz and *Spirituality and Spiritual Self-care: Expanding self-care deficit nursing theory* by White, Peters, & Schim was to report on the use of prayer or spirituality for patient healing.

Kutz's article is extremely brief, about two pages excluding references and specifically focuses on the use of prayer. He provides a list of recent journals and journal articles that were published on prayer use in healthcare. Kutz also indicates through his review of the Larimore study that lack of personal faith should be considered a risk factor to an individual's health. He goes on to question if it is the health care providers' responsibility to tell patients that it is a good idea to pray for health. Kutz is questioning this from a malpractice perspective not a proselytizing perspective as the research trends indicate that there is a correlation between prayer and health.

I question that if it becomes the responsibility of the health care provider to inform patients about prayer would they have to inform them about all types of faith traditions that use prayer or from their own tradition? Yet, what if they do not believe in prayer, God, or any higher power? A doctor and nurse only have so much time, would another informative pamphlet suffice? However, it should be noted that alternative health practices are being used with allopathic medicine. For example, Smilow Cancer Center has an outdoor mediation garden on an upper floor patio, the radiation waiting room has a huge fish tank with tropical fish to help patients relax, a nutritionist is available but they are not talking about plant-based diets (that is another discussion), Reiki, and massages (hot stones, etc.) are also available to patients at Smilow Cancer Center at Yale New Haven Hospital.

The article by White, et al. defines the difference between religion and spirituality and during their research process they came up with their own definition for spirituality that consists of two distinct concepts *spirituality and spiritual self-care.* The authors state that *"spirituality is defined as the beliefs a person holds related to a subjective sense of existential connectedness including beliefs that reflect relationships with others, acknowledging a higher power, recognizing an individual's place in the world, and lead to spiritual practices."* This gets at the idea of spirituality that is inclusive and leaves out any reference to a specific religion (Buddhism, Catholicism, etc.,). The authors then stated *"spiritual self-care is the set of spiritually-based practices in which people engage to promote continued personal development and well-being in times of health and illness."* The goal of this article is to expand on the nursing theory of Self-care deficit nursing theory or SCDNT. This is a theory that pushes self-care and the best ways to identify and empower ways that a patient can have advocacy over their own health. Using myself as an example, I do use prayer and spiritual practices as a way to advocate for myself not only praying for me but also for my health care team, and not just for my personal health, but that their personal lives are "blessed." I believe in energy and negative energy follows people, I do not want the negative energy from my surgeon not having a good day having an impact on my procedure.

White, et al. provided a diagram in the original article that would help in understanding the relationship between SCDNT and spirituality. I have listed the information briefly for your review on the next page in regard to the Basic Conditioning Factors that influence both Therapeutic Self-care Demand and Self-care Agency, which all impact an individuals overall health and well being. It is important to note that the authors of the study recognized environmental factors as an area that influences health, but did not indicate what was specifically included in that factor and the other basic conditioning factors[1]. Please read the original article for further information.

Basic Conditioning Factors
➤ Age
➤ Gender
➤ Developmental State
➤ Health Stats
➤ Family System Factors
➤ *Environmental Factors*
➤ Resource Availability
➤ Pattern of Living
➤ Sociocultural Orientation
➤ **Religious Affiliation**

Therapeutic Self-Care Demand
➤ Universal Requisites
➤ Developmental Requisites
➤ Health Deviation Requisites

Self Care Agency
➤ Self-Care Operations
➤ Power Components
➤ Basic Capabilities & Foundational Dispositions
➤ Value Hierarchy
➤ **Spirituality**

Self-Care
➤ Health Deviation
➤ Health Maintenance
➤ Health Promoting
➤ Growth & Development
➤ **Spiritual Self-Care**

Over Arching goal is Health & Well Being

Both articles are in agreement on two key issues. First, spirituality/prayer (not being used interchangeably here) are important variables that patients use for their health and wellness. Second, there is a role for the healthcare provider in accepting, understanding, and possibly informing patients that spirituality/prayer can play a vital role in their health outcomes. There are many more articles by medical professionals that acknowledge the existence of the correlation between spirituality and better health outcomes for some patients. I strongly believe we need to say what God said and do what Jesus said and did when it comes to our health. Remember there was a doctor among the disciples.

---

[1] This level of detail was not supplied in the article. It is suggested that you read both articles and others like them for more information.

CHAPTER THREE
WHAT GOD SAID

Remember Romans 10:17 *"So then faith cometh by hearing, and hearing by the word of God."*

I pose the following questions regarding healing: "How do we know whether it's God's will to heal us or not?" What did God say about healing? These are the same questions that many of us ask ourselves on a daily basis, and it does not matter if we are asking these questions for ourselves or for someone that we care about. We want to know what God says about healing and if He truly wants us healed. It does not matter what anyone else has to say about it. I would suggest that you use this list along with your favorite Bible translation to internalize and personalize God's word for yourself. In addition to the King James Version of the Bible I sometimes use the following translations: The Message Bible, the NIV (New International Version), the Amplified, or the New King James Version. The various versions use different words that can help clarify meaning. Using a good study Bible, a commentary, a concordance, and Bible dictionary are also useful.

> *"Study to shew thyself approved unto God, a workman that needeth not to be ashamed, rightly dividing the word of truth."*
>
> *2 Timothy 2:15*

I will break this list down for you into more manageable sections in the following chapters to help guide you along.

So you will see some of these same scriptures in the following chapters.

101 Things God Said
What did God say?
God said...
<u>Old Testament</u>

1. I am the Lord that healeth thee (Exodus 15:26).
2. Your days shall be one hundred and twenty years (Genesis 6:3).
3. You shall be buried in a good old age (Genesis 15:15).
4. You shall come to your grave in a full age like as a shock of corn cometh in his season (Job 5:26).
5. When I see the blood, I will pass over you and the plague shall not be upon you to destroy you (Exodus 12:13).
6. I will take sickness away from the midst of you and the number of your days I will fulfill (Exodus 23:25, 26).
7. I will not put any of the diseases you are afraid of on you, but I will take all sickness away from you (Deuteronomy 7:15).
8. It will be well with you and your days shall be multiplied and prolonged as the days of heaven upon the earth (Deuteronomy 11:9, 21).
9. I turned the curse into a blessing unto you, because I loved you (Deuteronomy 23:5 and Nehemiah 13:2).
10. I have redeemed you from every sickness and every plague (Deuteronomy 28:61 and Galatians 3:13).
11. As your days, so shall your strength be (Deuteronomy 33:25).

12. I have found a ransom for you, your flesh shall be fresher than a child's and you shall return to the days of your youth (Job 33:24, 25).
13. I have healed you and brought up your soul from the grave; I have kept you alive from going down into the pit (Psalms 30:1, 2).
14. I will give you strength and bless you with peace (Psalms 29:11).
15. I will preserve you and keep you alive (Psalms 41:2).
16. I will strengthen you upon the bed of languishing; I will turn all your bed in your sickness (Psalms 41:3).
17. I am the health of your countenance and your God (Psalms 43:5).
18. No plague shall come near your dwelling (Psalms 91:10).
19. I will satisfy you with long life (Psalms 91:16).
20. I heal all your diseases (Psalms 103:3)
21. I sent My word and healed you and delivered you from your destructions (Psalms 107:20).
22. You shall not die, but live, and declare My works (Psalms 118:17).
23. I heal your broken heart and bind up your wounds (Psalms 147:3).
24. The years of your life shall be many (Proverbs 4:10).
25. Trusting Me brings health to your navel and marrow to your bones (Proverbs 3:8).
26. My words are life to you, and health/medicine to all your flesh (Proverbs 4:22).
27. (My) good report makes your bones fat (Proverbs 15:30).
28. (My) pleasant words are sweet to your soul and health to your bones (Proverbs 16:24).
29. My joy is your strength. A merry heart does good like a medicine (Nehemiah 8:10; Proverbs 17:22).

30. The eyes of the blind shall be opened. The eyes of them that see shall not be dim (Isaiah 32:3; 35:5).

31. The ears of the deaf shall be unstopped. The ears of them that hear shall hearken (Isaiah 32:3; 35:5).

32. The tongue of the dumb shall sing. The tongue of the stammerers shall be ready to speak plainly (Isaiah 35:6; 32:4).

33. The lame man shall leap as a hart (Isaiah 35:6).

34. I will recover you and make you to live. I am ready to save you (Isaiah 38:16, 20).

35. I give power to the faint. I increase strength to them that have no might (Isaiah 40:29).

36. I will renew your strength. I will strengthen and help you (Isaiah 40:31; 41:10).

37. To your old age and gray hairs I will carry you and I will deliver you (Isaiah 46:4).

38. I bore your sickness (Isaiah 53:4).

39. I carried your pains (Isaiah 53:4).

40. I was put to sickness for you (Isaiah 53:10).

41. With My stripes you are healed (Isaiah 53:5).

42. I will heal you (Isaiah 57:19).

43. Your light shall break forth as the morning and your health shall spring forth speedily (Isaiah 58:8).

44. I will restore health unto you, and I will heal you of your wounds saith the Lord (Jeremiah 30:17).

45. Behold I will bring it health and cure, and I will cure you, and will reveal unto you the abundance of peace and truth (Jeremiah 33:6).

46. I will bind up that which was broken and will strengthen that which was sick (Ezekiel 34:16).

47. Behold, I will cause breath to enter into you and you shall live. And I shall put My Spirit in you and you shall live (Ezekiel 37:5, 14).

48. Whithersoever the rivers shall come shall live. They shall be healed and every thing shall live where the river comes (Ezekiel 47:9).
49. Seek Me and you shall live (Amos 5:4, 6).
50. I have arisen with healing in My wings (beams) (Malachi 4:2).

What did God say?
God said...
<u>New Testament</u>

51. I will, be thou clean (St. Matthew 8:3).
52. I took your infirmities (St. Matthew 8:17).
53. I bore your sicknesses (St. Matthew 8:17).
54. If you're sick you need a physician. (I am the Lord your physician) (St. Matthew 9:12 and Exodus 15:26).
55. I am moved with compassion toward the sick and I heal them (St. Matthew 14:14).
56. I heal all manner of sickness and all manner of disease (St. Matthew 4:23).
57. According to your faith, be it unto you (St. Matthew 9:29).
58. I give you power and authority over all unclean spirits to cast them out, and to heal all manner of sickness and all manner of disease (St. Matthew 10:1 and St. Luke 9:1).
59. I heal them all (St. Matthew 12:15 and Hebrews 13:8).
60. As many as touch Me are made perfectly whole (St. Matthew 14:36).
61. Healing is the children's bread (St. Matthew 15:26).
62. I do all things well. I make the deaf to hear and the dumb to speak (St. Mark 7:37).

63. If you can believe, all things are possible to him that believeth (St. Mark 9:23; 11:23, 24).

64. When hands are laid on you, you shall recover (St. Mark 16:18).

65. My anointing heals the brokenhearted, and delivers the captives, recovers sight to the blind, and sets at liberty those that are bruised (St. Luke 4:18; Isaiah 10:27; 61:1).

66. I heal all those who have need of healing (St. Luke 9:11).

67. I am not come to destroy men's lives but to save them (St. Luke 9:56).

68. Behold, I give you authority over all the enemy's power and nothing shall by any means hurt you (St. Luke 10:19).

69. Sickness is satanic bondage and you ought to be loosed today (St. Luke 13:16; 2 Corinthians 6:2).

70. In Me is life (St. John 1:4).

71. I am the bread of life. I give you life (St. John 6:33, 35).

72. The words I speak unto you are spirit and life (St. John 6:63).

73. I am come that you might have life, and that you might have it more abundantly (John 10:10).

74. I am the resurrection and the life (St. John 11:25).

75. If you ask anything in My name, I will do it (St. John 14:14).

76. Faith in My name makes you strong and gives you perfect soundness (Acts 3:16).

77. I stretch forth My hand to heal (Acts 4:30).

78. I, Jesus Christ, make you whole (Acts 9:34).

79. I do good and heal all that are oppressed of the devil (Acts 10:38).

80. My power causes diseases to depart from you (Acts 19:12).
81. The law of the Spirit of life in Me has made you free from the law of sin and death (Romans 8:2).
82. The same Spirit that raised Me from the dead now lives in you and that Spirit will quicken your mortal body (Romans 8:11).
83. Your body is a member of Me (1 Corinthians 6:15).
84. Your body is the temple of My Spirit and you're to glorify Me in your body (1 Corinthians 6:19, 20).
85. If you'll rightly discern My body which was broken for you, and judge yourself, you'll not be judged and you'll not be weak, sickly or die prematurely (1 Corinthians 11:29-31).
86. I have set gifts of healing in My body (1 Corinthians 12:9).
87. My life may be made manifest in your mortal flesh (2 Corinthians 4:10, 11).
88. I have delivered you from death, I do deliver you, and if you trust Me I will yet deliver you (2 Corinthians 1:10).
89. I have given you My name and have put all things under your feet (Ephesians 1:21, 22).
90. I want it to be well with you and I want you to live long on the earth. (Ephesians 6:3).
91. I have delivered you from the authority of darkness (Colossians 1:13).
92. I will deliver you from every evil work (2 Timothy 4:18).
93. I tasted death for you. I destroyed the devil who had the power of death. I've delivered you from the fear of death and bondage (Hebrews 2:9, 14, 15).
94. I wash your body with pure water (Hebrews 10:22; Ephesians 5:26).

95. Lift up the weak hands and the feeble knees. Don't let that which is lame be turned aside but rather let Me heal it (Hebrews 12:12, 13).
96. Let the elders anoint you and pray for you in My name and I will raise you up (James 5:14, 15).
97. Pray for one another and I will heal you (James 5:16).
98. By My stripes you were healed (1 Peter 2:24).
99. My Divine power has given unto you all things that pertain unto life and godliness through the knowledge of Me (2 Peter 1:3).
100. Whosoever will let him come and take of the water of life freely (Revelation 22:17).
101. Beloved, I wish above all things that you may...be in health (3 John 2).

CHAPTER FOUR
WHAT JESUS DID

It is impossible to read any one of the Gospels, beginning to end, and not encounter the stories of healing or miracles performed by Jesus and his disciples. Jesus is witnessed as the One who restores health and identity to individuals through their encounters with Him. In St. John 14:12 Jesus states that: "Verily, verily, I say unto you, he that believeth on me, the works that I do shall he do also; and greater works than these shall he do; because I go unto my Father." This is without question evidence of the promise to his disciples and to us that we can do what Jesus did.

The Book of Acts recounts further evidence of healing after the resurrection and ascension of Jesus. The Biblical record seems quite clear; a ministry of healing was one of the principle ways the church grew and souls were saved in the first decades and centuries of the church. It is still a tool for today.

Review the healing stories and pay close attention to the common thread of faith:

Lazarus Raised –

St. John 11:1- 44 Now a certain man was sick, named Lazarus, of Bethany, the town of Mary and her sister Martha. (It was that Mary which anointed the Lord with ointment, and wiped his feet with her hair, whose brother Lazarus was sick.) Therefore his sisters sent unto him, saying, Lord, behold, he whom thou lovest is sick. When Jesus heard that, he said, This sickness is not unto death, but for the glory of God, that the Son of God might be glorified thereby. Now Jesus loved Martha, and her sister, and Lazarus.When he had heard therefore that he was sick, he abode two days still in the same place where he was. Then after that saith he to his disciples, Let us go into Judaea again. His disciples say unto him, Master, the Jews of late sought to stone thee; and goest thou thither again? Jesus answered, Are there not twelve hours in the day? If any man walk in the day, he stumbleth not, because he seeth the light of this world. But if a man walk in the night, he stumbleth, because there is no light in him. These things said he: and after that he saith unto them, Our friend Lazarus sleepeth; but I go, that I may awake him out of sleep. Then said his disciples, Lord, if he sleep, he shall do well. Howbeit Jesus spake of his death: but they thought that he had spoken of taking of rest in sleep. Then said Jesus unto them plainly, Lazarus is dead. And I am glad for your sakes that I was not there, to the intent ye may believe; nevertheless let us go unto him. Then said Thomas, which is called Didymus, unto his fellow disciples, Let us also go, that we may die with him. Then when Jesus came, he found that he had lain in the grave four days already. Now Bethany was nigh unto Jerusalem, about fifteen furlongs off: And many of the Jews came to Martha and Mary, to comfort them concerning their brother. Then Martha, as soon as she heard that Jesus was coming, went and met him: but Mary sat still in the house.

Then said Martha unto Jesus, Lord, if thou hadst been here, my brother had not died. But I know, that even now, whatsoever thou wilt ask of God, God will give it thee. Jesus saith unto her, Thy brother shall rise again. Martha saith unto him, I know that he shall rise again in the resurrection at the last day. Jesus said unto her, I am the resurrection, and the life: he that believeth in me, though he were dead, yet shall he live: And whosoever liveth and believeth in me shall never die. Believest thou this? She saith unto him, Yea, Lord: I believe that thou art the Christ, the Son of God, which should come into the world. And when she had so said, she went her way, and called Mary her sister secretly, saying, The Master is come, and calleth for thee. As soon as she heard that, she arose quickly, and came unto him. Now Jesus was not yet come into the town, but was in that place where Martha met him. The Jews then which were with her in the house, and comforted her, when they saw Mary, that she rose up hastily and went out, followed her, saying, She goeth unto the grave to weep there.

Then when Mary was come where Jesus was, and saw him, she fell down at his feet, saying unto him, Lord, if thou hadst been here, my brother had not died. When Jesus therefore saw her weeping, and the Jews also weeping which came with her, he groaned in the spirit, and was troubled. And said, Where have ye laid him? They said unto him, Lord, come and see. Jesus wept.

Then said the Jews, Behold how he loved him! And some of them said, Could not this man, which opened the eyes of the blind, have caused that even this man should not have died? Jesus therefore again groaning in himself cometh to the grave. It was a cave, and a stone lay upon it. Jesus said, Take ye away the stone. Martha, the sister of him that was dead, saith unto him, Lord, by this time he stinketh: for he hath been dead four days.

Jesus saith unto her, Said I not unto thee, that, if thou wouldest believe, thou shouldest see the glory of God? Then they took away the stone from the place where the dead was laid. And Jesus lifted up his eyes, and said, Father, I thank thee that thou hast heard me. And I knew that thou hearest me always: but because of the people which stand by I said it, that they may believe that thou hast sent me. And when he thus had spoken, he cried with a loud voice, Lazarus, come forth. And he that was dead came forth, bound hand and foot with grave clothes: and his face was bound about with a napkin. Jesus saith unto them, Loose him, and let him go.

Lepers Healed -
St. Luke 17:11-19 And it came to pass, as he went to Jerusalem, that he passed through the midst of Samaria and Galilee. And as he

entered into a certain village, there met him ten men that were lepers, which stood afar off: And they lifted up their voices, and said, Jesus, Master, have mercy on us. And when he saw them, he said unto them, Go shew yourselves unto the priests. And it came to pass, that, as they went, they were cleansed. And one of them, when he saw that he was healed, turned back, and with a loud voice glorified God, And fell down on his face at his feet, giving him thanks: and he was a Samaritan. And Jesus answering said, Were there not ten cleansed? But where are the nine? There are not found that returned to give glory to God, save this stranger. And he said unto him, Arise, go thy way: thy faith hath made thee whole.

Deaf Heard, Blind See, Lepers Healed -

St. John 11:5 The blind receive their sight, and the lame walk, the lepers are cleansed, and the deaf hear, the dead are raised up, and the poor have the gospel preached to them.

Cast out Devils -

St. Matthew 9:31-35 But they, when they were departed, spread abroad his fame in all that country. As they went out, behold, they brought to him a dumb man possessed with a devil. And when the devil was cast out, the dumb spake: and the multitudes marvelled, saying, It was never so seen in Israel. But the Pharisees said, He casteth out devils through the prince of the devils. And Jesus went

about all the cities and villages, teaching in
their synagogues, and preaching the gospel of
the kingdom, and healing every sickness and
every disease among the people.

Here are additional references related to the healing acts of
Jesus while he was here on earth. Read and study for
yourself.

St. Matthew 4:23, 24	St. Luke 4:16-21
St. Matthew 8:2, 3	St. Luke 4:33-36
St. Matthew 8:5-10, 13	St. Luke 4:40, 41
	St. Luke 6:6-10
St. Matthew 8:14-17	St. Luke 6:17-19
St. Matthew 9:20-22	St. Luke 13:11-17
St. Matthew 9:27-36	St. John 5:2-14
St. Matthew 11:28-30	St. John 9:1-7
St. Matthew 12:15	St. John 10:10
St. Matthew 14:13, 14	Acts 10:38
St. Matthew 14:34-36	Hebrews 13:8
St. Matthew 15:29-31	1John 3:8
St. Mark 5:1-43	St. Matthew 10:1
St. Mark 6:53-56	St. Mark 16:15-20
St. Mark 7:25-37	
St. Mark 9:17-29	

These are the healing works of the disciples done in Jesus
name. Read and study for yourself.

Lame Walked -
Acts 3:1-17 Now Peter and John went up
together into the temple at the hour of prayer,
being the ninth hour. And a certain man lame

from his mother's womb was carried, whom
they laid daily at the gate of the temple which
is called Beautiful, to ask alms of them that
entered into the temple; Who seeing Peter and
John about to go into the temple asked an
alms. And Peter, fastening his eyes upon him
with John, said, Look on us. And he gave
heed unto them, expecting to receive
something of them. Then Peter said, Silver
and gold have I none; but such as I have give
I thee: In the name of Jesus Christ of
Nazareth rise up and walk. And he took him
by the right hand, and lifted him up: and
immediately his feet and ankle bones received
strength. And he leaping up stood, and
walked, and entered with them into the
temple, walking, and leaping, and praising
God. And all the people saw him walking and
praising God: And they knew that it was he
which sat for alms at the Beautiful gate of the
temple: and they were filled with wonder and
amazement at that which had happened unto
him. And as the lame man which was healed
held Peter and John, all the people ran
together unto them in the porch that is called
Solomon's, greatly wondering. And when
Peter saw it, he answered unto the people, Ye
men of Israel, why marvel ye at this? or why
look ye so earnestly on us, as though by our
own power or holiness we had made this man
to walk? The God of Abraham, and of Isaac,
and of Jacob, the God of our fathers, hath
glorified his Son Jesus; whom ye delivered up,
and denied him in the presence of Pilate,

when he was determined to let him go. But ye denied the Holy One and the Just, and desired a murderer to be granted unto you; And killed the Prince of life, whom God hath raised from the dead; whereof we are witnesses. And his name through faith in his name hath made this man strong, whom ye see and know: yea, the faith which is by him hath given him this perfect soundness in the presence of you all. And now, brethren, I wot that through ignorance ye did it, as did also your rulers.

Additional references:

St. John 14:12-15	Acts 14:8-10
Acts 6:8	Acts 19:11, 12
Acts 8:6, 7	James 5:14-16
Acts 9:33, 34	

CHAPTER FIVE
BELIEVE THIS

"Suffering is universal for mankind. There is no one who escapes."

Howard Thurman

"My God, my God, why hast thou forsaken me? Why art thou so far from helping me, and from the words of my roaring (groans, sighs of agony)? O my God, I cry in the daytime, but thou hearest not; and in the night season, and am not silent."

Psalms 22:1-3

Most Christians do not by nature consider suffering a privilege. Yet when we suffer if we faithfully represent Christ, our message and example affect others and us for good (see Acts 5:41). Paul considered it a privilege to suffer for Christ and when we suffer for our faith, it does not mean that we have done something wrong. During my research to answer the question: Why me Lord? Why me? I had to look at the role of suffering in Christian living and life in general. I turned my attention to the writings of Howard Thurman[1], specifically Disciplines of the Spirit (1963).

The idea and role of suffering was not something that I accepted right away. I was like many who are sick with disease and I kept trying to figure out if my punishment fit the crime. What had I done in my life that was so awful that my physical body would turn against me in such a terrible way? Some people get stuck in the fire and brimstone of the Old Testament. I know I did. I spent many hours trying to compute the crime and punishment equation. Reflecting on the transgressions of my youth and wondering why me? Why did I get cancer? I did not think this punishment was just by my calculation. I thought I was average in the obedience area and a pretty good kid. I felt suffering through cancer, having a near death experience, and living with the subsequent physical and psychological aftermath did not equal any crime that I could have committed. Thurman helped me to understand that there is nothing that anyone can do when it comes to the role of suffering and the human condition. It happens to everyone, good, bad or indifferent. What we have to remember is that Jesus came to redeem us from the curse of the law found in Deuteronomy 28. That is what we all have to remember. We have to grab hold of what the Bible says in Galatians 3:13:

> *"Christ purchased our freedom [redeeming us] from the curse (doom) of the Law [and its condemnation] by [Himself] becoming a curse for us, for it is written [in the Scriptures], Cursed is everyone who hangs on a tree (is crucified)."*

Deuteronomy 28
The Curse of the Law and Blessings for Obedience

And it shall come to pass, if thou shalt hearken diligently unto the voice of the Lord

27

thy God, to observe and to do all his
commandments which I command thee this
day, that the Lord thy God will set thee on
high above all nations of the earth: And all
these blessings shall come on thee, and
overtake thee, if thou shalt hearken unto the
voice of the Lord thy God. Blessed shalt thou
be in the city, and blessed shalt thou be in the
field. Blessed shall be the fruit of thy body,
and the fruit of thy ground, and the fruit of
thy cattle, the increase of thy kine, and the
flocks of thy sheep. Blessed shall be thy
basket and thy store. Blessed shalt thou be
when thou comest in, and blessed shalt thou
be when thou goest out.

The Lord shall cause thine enemies that rise
up against thee to be smitten before thy face:
they shall come out against thee one way, and
flee before thee seven ways. The Lord shall
command the blessing upon thee in thy
storehouses, and in all that thou settest thine
hand unto; and He shall bless thee in the land
which the Lord thy God giveth thee. The
Lord shall establish thee an holy people unto
Himself, as He hath sworn unto thee, if thou
shalt keep the commandments of the Lord
thy God, and walk in His ways. And all people
of the earth shall see that thou art called by

the name of the Lord; and they shall be afraid of thee. And the Lord shall make thee plenteous in goods, in the fruit of thy body, and in the fruit of thy cattle, and in the fruit of thy ground, in the land which the Lord sware unto thy fathers to give thee. The Lord shall open unto thee His good treasure, the heaven to give the rain unto thy land in His season, and to bless all the work of thine hand: and thou shalt lend unto many nations, and thou shalt not borrow.

And the Lord shall make thee the head, and not the tail; and thou shalt be above only, and thou shalt not be beneath; if that thou hearken unto the commandments of the Lord thy God, which I command thee this day, to observe and to do them: And thou shalt not go aside from any of the words which I command thee this day, to the right hand, or to the left, to go after other gods to serve them. But it shall come to pass, if thou wilt not hearken unto the voice of the Lord thy God, to observe to do all his commandments and his statutes which I command thee this day; that all these curses shall come upon thee, and overtake thee: Cursed shalt thou be in the city, and cursed shalt thou be in the field. Cursed shall be thy basket and thy store.

Cursed shall be the fruit of thy body, and the fruit of thy land, the increase of thy kine, and the flocks of thy sheep. Cursed shalt thou be when thou comest in, and cursed shalt thou be when thou goest out.

The Lord shall send upon thee cursing, vexation, and rebuke, in all that thou settest thine hand unto for to do, until thou be destroyed, and until thou perish quickly; because of the wickedness of thy doings, whereby thou hast forsaken me. The Lord shall make the pestilence cleave unto thee, until he have consumed thee from off the land, whither thou goest to possess it. The Lord shall smite thee with a consumption, and with a fever, and with an inflammation, and with an extreme burning, and with the sword, and with blasting, and with mildew; and they shall pursue thee until thou perish. And thy heaven that is over thy head shall be brass, and the earth that is under thee shall be iron.

The Lord shall make the rain of thy land powder and dust: from heaven shall it come down upon thee, until thou be destroyed. The Lord shall cause thee to be smitten before thine enemies: thou shalt go out one way against them, and flee seven ways before

them: and shalt be removed into all the
kingdoms of the earth. And thy carcass shall
be meat unto all fowls of the air, and unto the
beasts of the earth, and no man shall fray
them away.

The Lord will smite thee with the botch of
Egypt, and with the emerods, and with the
scab, and with the itch, whereof thou canst
not be healed. The Lord shall smite thee with
madness, and blindness, and astonishment of
heart: And thou shalt grope at noonday, as the
blind gropeth in darkness, and thou shalt not
prosper in thy ways: and thou shalt be only
oppressed and spoiled evermore, and no man
shall save thee. Thou shalt betroth a wife, and
another man shall lie with her: thou shalt
build an house, and thou shalt not dwell
therein: thou shalt plant a vineyard, and shalt
not gather the grapes thereof. Thine ox shall
be slain before thine eyes, and thou shalt not
eat thereof: thine ass shall be violently taken
away from before thy face, and shall not be
restored to thee: thy sheep shall be given unto
thine enemies, and thou shalt have none to
rescue them.

Thy sons and thy daughters shall be given
unto another people, and thine eyes shall

look, and fail with longing for them all the day long; and there shall be no might in thine hand. The fruit of thy land, and all thy labours, shall a nation which thou knowest not eat up; and thou shalt be only oppressed and crushed alway: So that thou shalt be mad for the sight of thine eyes which thou shalt see.

The Lord shall smite thee in the knees, and in the legs, with a sore botch that cannot be healed, from the sole of thy foot unto the top of thy head. The Lord shall bring thee, and thy king which thou shalt set over thee, unto a nation which neither thou nor thy fathers have known; and there shalt thou serve other gods, wood and stone. And thou shalt become an astonishment, a proverb, and a byword, among all nations whither the Lord shall lead thee. Thou shalt carry much seed out into the field, and shalt gather but little in; for the locust shall consume it.

Thou shalt plant vineyards, and dress them, but shalt neither drink of the wine, nor gather the grapes; for the worms shall eat them. Thou shalt have olive trees throughout all thy coasts, but thou shalt not anoint thyself with the oil; for thine olive shall cast his fruit.

Thou shalt beget sons and daughters, but thou
shalt not enjoy them; for they shall go into
captivity. All thy trees and fruit of thy land
shall the locust consume. The stranger that is
within thee shall get up above thee very high;
and thou shalt come down very low. He shall
lend to thee, and thou shalt not lend to him:
he shall be the head, and thou shalt be the tail.
Moreover all these curses shall come upon
thee, and shall pursue thee, and overtake thee,
till thou be destroyed; because thou
hearkenedst not unto the voice of the Lord
thy God, to keep his commandments and his
statutes which he commanded thee: And they
shall be upon thee for a sign and for a
wonder, and upon thy seed for ever. Because
thou servedst not the Lord thy God with
joyfulness, and with gladness of heart, for the
abundance of all things; Therefore shalt thou
serve thine enemies which the Lord shall send
against thee, in hunger, and in thirst, and in
nakedness, and in want of all things: and he
shall put a yoke of iron upon thy neck, until
he have destroyed thee.

The Lord shall bring a nation against thee
from far, from the end of the earth, as swift as
the eagle flieth; a nation whose tongue thou

shalt not understand; A nation of fierce
countenance, which shall not regard the
person of the old, nor shew favour to the
young: And he shall eat the fruit of thy cattle,
and the fruit of thy land, until thou be
destroyed: which also shall not leave thee
either corn, wine, or oil, or the increase of thy
kine, or flocks of thy sheep, until he have
destroyed thee. And he shall besiege thee in all
thy gates, until thy high and fenced walls
come down, wherein thou trustedst,
throughout all thy land: and he shall besiege
thee in all thy gates throughout all thy land,
which the Lord thy God hath given thee.
And thou shalt eat the fruit of thine own
body, the flesh of thy sons and of thy
daughters, which the Lord thy God hath given
thee, in the siege, and in the straitness,
wherewith thine enemies shall distress thee:
So that the man that is tender among you, and
very delicate, his eye shall be evil toward his
brother, and toward the wife of his bosom,
and toward the remnant of his children which
he shall leave: So that he will not give to any
of them of the flesh of his children whom he
shall eat: because he hath nothing left him in
the siege, and in the straitness, wherewith
thine enemies shall distress thee in all thy
gates.

The tender and delicate woman among you, which would not adventure to set the sole of her foot upon the ground for delicateness and tenderness, her eye shall be evil toward the husband of her bosom, and toward her son, and toward her daughter, And toward her young one that cometh out from between her feet, and toward her children which she shall bear: for she shall eat them for want of all things secretly in the siege and straitness, wherewith thine enemy shall distress thee in thy gates. If thou wilt not observe to do all the words of this law that are written in this book, that thou mayest fear this glorious and fearful name, The Lord Thy God; Then the Lord will make thy plagues wonderful, and the plagues of thy seed, even great plagues, and of long continuance, and sore sicknesses, and of long continuance. Moreover he will bring upon thee all the diseases of Egypt, which thou wast afraid of; and they shall cleave unto thee. Also every sickness, and every plague, which is not written in the book of this law, them will the Lord bring upon thee, until thou be destroyed. And ye shall be left few in number, whereas ye were as the stars of heaven for multitude; because thou wouldest not obey the voice of the Lord thy God.

And it shall come to pass, that as the Lord rejoiced over you to do you good, and to multiply you; so the Lord will rejoice over you to destroy you, and to bring you to nought; and ye shall be plucked from off the land whither thou goest to possess it. And the Lord shall scatter thee among all people, from the one end of the earth even unto the other; and there thou shalt serve other gods, which neither thou nor thy fathers have known, even wood and stone. And among these nations shalt thou find no ease, neither shall the sole of thy foot have rest: but the Lord shall give thee there a trembling heart, and failing of eyes, and sorrow of mind: And thy life shall hang in doubt before thee; and thou shalt fear day and night, and shalt have none assurance of thy life: In the morning thou shalt say, Would God it were even! and at even thou shalt say, Would God it were morning! for the fear of thine heart wherewith thou shalt fear, and for the sight of thine eyes which thou shalt see. And the Lord shall bring thee into Egypt again with ships, by the way whereof I spake unto thee, Thou shalt see it no more again: and there ye shall be sold unto your enemies for bondmen and bondwomen, and no man shall buy you.

Proverbs 29:18 Obedience

Where there is no vision, the people perish:
but he that keepeth the law, happy is he.

Galatians 3 We Have Been Redeemed Have Faith

O foolish Galatians, who hath bewitched you,
that ye should not obey the truth, before
whose eyes Jesus Christ hath been evidently
set forth, crucified among you? This only
would I learn of you, Received ye the Spirit by
the works of the law, or by the hearing of
faith? Are ye so foolish? Having begun in the
Spirit, are ye now made perfect by the flesh?
Have ye suffered so many things in vain? if it
be yet in vain. He therefore that ministereth
to you the Spirit, and worketh miracles among
you, doeth he it by the works of the law, or by
the hearing of faith?

Even as Abraham believed God, and it was
accounted to him for righteousness. Know ye
therefore that they, which are of faith, the
same, are the children of Abraham. And the
scripture, foreseeing that God would justify
the heathen through faith, preached before
the gospel unto Abraham, saying, In thee shall
all nations be blessed. So then they, which be
of faith, are blessed with faithful Abraham.

For as many as are of the works of the law are under the curse: for it is written, Cursed is every one that continueth not in all things, which are written in the book of the law to do them.

But that no man is justified by the law in the sight of God, it is evident: for, The just shall live by faith. And the law is not of faith: but, The man that doeth them shall live in them. Christ hath redeemed us from the curse of the law, being made a curse for us: for it is written, Cursed is every one that hangeth on a tree: That the blessing of Abraham might come on the Gentiles through Jesus Christ; that we might receive the promise of the Spirit through faith. Brethren, I speak after the manner of men; Though it be but a man's covenant, yet if it be confirmed, no man disannulleth, or addeth thereto.

Now to Abraham and his seed were the promises made. He saith not, And to seeds, as of many; but as of one, And to thy seed, which is Christ. And this I say, that the covenant, that was confirmed before of God in Christ, the law, which was four hundred and thirty years after, cannot disannul, that it should make the promise of none effect. For

if the inheritance be of the law, it is no more
of promise: but God gave it to Abraham by
promise. Wherefore then serveth the law? It
was added because of transgressions, till the
seed should come to whom the promise was
made; and it was ordained by angels in the
hand of a mediator. Now a mediator is not a
mediator of one, but God is one. Is the law
then against the promises of God? God
forbid: for if there had been a law given which
could have given life, verily righteousness
should have been by the law.

But the scripture hath concluded all under sin,
that the promise by faith of Jesus Christ might
be given to them that believe. But before
faith came, we were kept under the law, shut
up unto the faith which should afterwards be
revealed. Wherefore the law was our
schoolmaster to bring us unto Christ, that we
might be justified by faith. But after that faith
is come, we are no longer under a
schoolmaster. For ye are all the children of
God by faith in Christ Jesus. For as many of
you as have been baptized into Christ have
put on Christ. There is neither Jew nor Greek,
there is neither bond nor free, there is neither
male nor female: for ye are all one in Christ
Jesus. And if ye be Christ's, then are ye

Abraham's seed, and heirs according to the promise.

We are no longer bound and cursed by the law! We have been saved! We have been redeemed!

---

[1] **Howard Thurman** (November 18, 1899 – April 10, 1981) was an influential African American author, philosopher, theologian, educator and civil rights leader. He was Dean of Chapel at Howard University and Boston for more than two decades, wrote 21 books, and in 1944 helped found a multicultural church. He along with Mordecai Johnson and Vernon Johns was considered one of the three greatest African-American preachers in the early 20th-century.

CHAPTER SIX
SPIRITUAL WARFARE

"Finally, my brethren, be strong in the Lord, and in the power of his might. Put on the whole armour of God, that ye may be able to stand against the wiles of the devil. For we wrestle not against flesh and blood, but against principalities, against powers, against the rulers of the darkness of this world, against spiritual wickedness in high places. Wherefore take unto you the whole armour of God, that ye may be able to withstand in the evil day, and having done all, to stand. Stand therefore, having your loins girt about with truth, and having on the breastplate of righteousness; And your feet shod with the preparation of the gospel of peace; Above all, taking the shield of faith, wherewith ye shall be able to quench all the fiery darts of the wicked. And take the helmet of salvation, and the sword of the Spirit, which is the word of God: Praying always with all prayer and supplication in the Spirit, and watching thereunto with all perseverance and supplication for all saints; And for me, that utterance may be given unto me, that I may open my mouth boldly, to make known the mystery of the gospel, For which I am an ambassador in bonds: that therein I may speak boldly, as I ought to speak."

Ephesians 6:10-20

The biblical and spiritual principle of binding and loosing is used as a weapon of warfare against the enemy. It is a good idea to continue to study the word of God in this area particularly if you come from a conservative Christian background like I did. Personally, I did not grow up with the stereotypical Pentecostal or Charismatic religious background that one might associate with the belief in the biblical concept of binding, loosing, and spiritual warfare. I found it along my spiritual journey. Reading about it in the Bible and actually incorporating it into your prayer life is a different type of understanding that requires continued prayer and study. A popular book that has been around for a long time is called *Strongman's his name-What's his game? An Authoritative Biblical Approach to Spiritual Warfare* (1983) by Drs. Jerry and Carol Robeson.

Loose
St. Matthew 16:19

> And I will give unto thee the keys of the
> kingdom of heaven: and whatsoever thou
> shalt bind on earth shall be bound in heaven:
> and whatsoever thou shalt loose on earth shall
> be loosed in heaven.

Bind
St. Matthew 18:18

> Verily I say unto you, whatsoever ye shall bind
> on earth shall be bound in heaven: and
> whatsoever ye shall loose on earth shall be
> loosed in heaven.

Bind the spirit of infirmity
St. Luke 13:11-13, 16

> And, behold, there was a woman, which had a
> spirit of infirmity eighteen years, and was
> bowed together, and could in no wise lift up

42

herself. And when Jesus saw her, he called her to him, and said unto her, Woman, <u>thou art loosed</u> from thine infirmity. And he laid his hands on her: and immediately she was made straight, and glorified God. . . . . .And ought not this woman, being a daughter of Abraham, whom Satan hath bound, lo, these eighteen years, be loosed from this bond on the sabbath day?

Loose the Spirit of Life
Romans 8:1&2

There is therefore now no condemnation to them which are in Christ Jesus, who walk not after the flesh, but after the Spirit. For the law of <u>the Spirit of life</u> in Christ Jesus hath made me free from the law of sin and death.

Loose the Gifts of Healing
1 Corinthians 12:9

To another faith by the same Spirit; to another the gifts of healing by the same Spirit.
Remember: Pray without ceasing!

CHAPTER SEVEN
HOLD ON TO FAITH AND THE
PROMISES OF GOD

"Are you now going to accuse me of being flip with my promises because it didn't work out? Do you think I talk out of both sides of my mouth—a glib yes one moment, a glib no the next? Well, you're wrong. I try to be as true to my word as God is to His. Our word to you wasn't a careless yes canceled by an indifferent no. How could it be? When Silas and Timothy and I proclaimed the Son of God among you, did you pick up on any yes-and-no, on-again, off-again waffling? Wasn't it a clean, strong Yes?
Whatever God has promised gets stamped with the Yes of Jesus. In him, this is what we preach and pray, the great Amen, God's Yes and our Yes together, gloriously evident. God affirms us, making us a sure thing in Christ, putting his Yes within us. By his Spirit he has stamped us with his eternal pledge—a sure beginning of what he is destined to complete. Holding on to the promises of God in sickness and in health."

2 Corinthians 1:17-22 The Message (MSG)

One thing that has troubled me is my inability to consistently hold on to the promises of God. This will always be a work in progress. I am sure I am not the only

44

one who has had moments of doubt and wavering faith. This is particularly so when things are not going as well as planned or hoped for. Personally, I stay in what seems to me like a state of perpetual prayer, yet somehow doubt sets in. The Bible tells us of God's promises and what the ultimate outcome looks like yet we fail to hold on to the promises. Yes, I know we as human beings are imperfect and we fail so miserably, but we have to keep our eye on the ultimate prize. We are challenged at every turn by fear, doubt, and temptation. We are more than conquers, the Bible tells us so. We just have to activate our faith and walk in the promises of God. We have to stop focusing on the Law and focus on redemption. We are surrounded by sin and the repetition of messages about the wrathful God has an impact on our ability to hold on to the goodness of God. We have to always think on the things that are good (Philippians 4:8). Failing to hold on to the promises comes from not fully and consistently remembering the redemption story. You know the one where Jesus came so that we might have life and have it more abundantly.

When we study the healing works of Jesus and the disciples we have to consider who was on the other end. There were those seeking healing for someone else and those seeking healing for themselves both of which required faith. Even those with little or no faith confessed their inadequacy in this area and received the healing for themselves and/or their family member. You can too.

Have faith believe and accept your healing!
Malachi 4:2
Hebrews 1:1-4
Philippians 2:8-11
Ephesians 1:16:23

Remember that healing comes through the name of Jesus!
St. John 16:23,24
St. Mark 16:15-18
St. John 14:13,14
Acts 3:1-16
Acts 4:1-18
Acts 4:23,24,29,30

Receive your healing by faith!
St. Matthew 18:19
St. Mark 11:22-26
Romans 4:17,19-21
Romans 10:17
1 Timothy 6:12
Hebrews 11:1
Hebrews 11:6
1 John 5:4,5

Yes! God wants our bodies healed!
1 Corinthians 3:16
Romans 8:2
1 John 4:4

Romans 8:11

Philippians 2:13

James 4:7

2 Timothy 1:7

Hebrews 2:14,15

Romans 6:14

Confession Activates Your Faith

Hebrews 4:14-16

Hebrews 10:23

Hebrews 10:35,36

Philemon 1:6

Revelation 12:11

Joel 3:10

PRAY, PRAY, PRAY OR BE PREY!

CHAPTER EIGHT
A PRAYER FOR HEALING AND HEALTH

Father, in the name of Jesus, I confess Your Word concerning healing for my mind, body, and spirit. As I do this, I believe and say that Your Word will not return to You Void, but will accomplish what it says it will. Therefore, I believe in the name of Jesus that I am healed in mind, body, and spirit, according to 1 Peter 2:24. It is written in Your Word that Jesus Himself took our infirmities and bore our sicknesses. Therefore, with great boldness and confidence I say on the authority of the written Word that I am redeemed from the curse of sickness and dis-ease, and I refuse to tolerate its symptoms.

Satan, I speak to you in the name of Jesus and say that your principalities, powers, your spirits who rule the present darkness, and your spiritual wickedness in heavenly places are bound from operating against me in any way. I am the property of ALMIGHTY GOD, and I give you no place in me. I dwell in the secret place of the MOST HIGH GOD. I abide, remain stable and fixed under the shadow of the ALMIGHTY, whose power no foe can withstand.

Now, Father, because I reverence and worship YOU, I have the assurance of YOUR WORD that the angel of the

Lord encamps around about me and delivers me from every evil work. No evil shall befall me; no plague or calamity shall come near my dwelling. I confess the Word of God abides in me and delivers to me perfect soundness of mind and wholeness in body and spirit from the deepest parts of my nature in my immortal spirit even to the joints and marrow of my bones. The WORD is medication and life to my flesh for the law of the Spirit of Life operates in me and makes me free from the law of sin and death.

I have on the whole armor of God, and the shield of faith protects me from all the fiery darts of the wicked. Jesus is the High Priest of my confession, and I hold fast to my confession of faith in Your Word. I stand immovable and fixed in full assurance that I have health and healing in all three parts of my being, mental, physical, and spiritual; all now in the name of Jesus. Amen.

Once this has been prayed, thank the Father, thank Jesus, thank the Holy Spirit, that the enemy Satan is bound and continue to confess this healing and thank God for it, always![1]

Scripture References:

Isaiah 55:11	Psalms 91:10
1 Peter 2:24	Psalms 34:7
St. Matthew 8:17	2 Timothy 1:7
Galatians 3:13	Hebrews 4:12, 14
James 4:7	Proverbs 4:22

Ephesians 6:12	Romans 8:2
2 Corinthians 10:4	Ephesians 6:11, 16
Psalms 91:1	Psalms 112:7

Personalize this prayer. Be specific and name what you want God to heal you from. Remember we have to do our part and be active participants to be healthy physically, mentally and spiritually.

The information compiled in this booklet is for your use in continued biblical study.

---

[1] Based on a prayer written by Germaine Copeland for Prayers that Avail Much for Women Special Gift Addition, Harrison House Publishers, 1997 for Word Ministries, Inc.

BIBLIOGRAPHY

Bible King James Version. Public domain. Accessed 1/27/15. https://www.Biblegateway.com.

Brazee, M. (1999, 2003). Prescription for healing: 365 Daily devotions. Tulsa, OK: Harrison House.

Copeland, G. (1997). Prayers that avail much for women: Special gift addition. Tulsa, OK: Harrison House.

Garrison, M. (1976). How to try a spirit: Identifying evil spirits and the fruit they manifest. New Kensington, PA: Whitaker House.

Grant, J. (1989). White women's Christ and Black women's Jesus: Feminist Christology and Womanist Response. Academy Series No. 64. Atlanta, GA: Scholars Press.

Hagin, K. E. (1993). Healing scriptures. Tulsa, OK: Faith Library Publications.

Hollies, L. H. (1992). Inner healing for broken vessels: Seven steps to a woman's way of healing. Nashville, TN: Upper Room Books.

Kutz, M. R. (2004). Observations on prayer as a viable treatment intervention: A brief review for healthcare providers. *The Internet Journal of Allied Health Sciences and Practice. 2 (1).*

Moore, K. (2013). God's Will to Heal. Accessed 1/27/2015. http://www.flcmedia.org/books/Gods_Will_To_H eal_9-12-13/#207/z.

Murphy, E. (1992). The handbook of spiritual warfare. Nashville, TN: Thomas Nelson Publishers.

National Cancer Institute. BRCA1 and BRCA2. Accessed 1/27/2015. http://www.cancer.gov/cancertopics/factsheet/Ris k/BRCA.

National Cancer Institute. Managing chemotherapy side effects – Alopecia/Hair loss. Accessed 1/28/2015. http://www.cancer.gov/publications/patient-education/hairloss.pdf.

National Cancer Institute. Managing chemotherapy side effects – Memory changes. Accessed 1/28/2015. http://www.cancer.gov/publications/patient-education/memory.pdf.

National Cancer Institute. Managing chemotherapy side effects - Neuropathy. Accessed 1/28/2015. http://www.cancer.gov/publications/patient-education/nerve.pdf.

Peterson, E. H., (2002). The message Bible. Colorado Springs, CO: Nav Press Publishing Group.

Robeson, J. & Robeson, C. (1984). Strongman's his name - what's his game? An authoritative biblical approach to spiritual warfare. New Kensington, PA: Whitaker House.

Strong, J., Kohlenberger, J. R.,III, and Swanson, J. A. (2001). The strongest Strong's exhaustive concordance of the Bible. Grand Rapids, MI: Zondervan.

Thurman, H. (1963). Disciplines of the Spirit. Richmond, IN: Friends United Press.

White, M. L., Peters, R. & Myers Schim, S. (2011). Spirituality and Spiritual Self-care: Expanding self-care deficit nursing theory. *Nursing Science Quarterly, 24 (1), 48-46.*

ABOUT THE AUTHOR

Annette Madlock Gatison, Ph.D. is an independent scholar and Associate Professor. She completed her doctoral work at Howard University in Washington, DC. Madlock Gatison has also served in many leadership roles with the various churches she has been involved in.

Madlock Gatison's current research and writing, The Pink and The Black Project© focuses on the negotiation of identity and the spiral of silence as it relates to women's health; the communicative practices of breast cancer survivors, their family and friends. To ground and inform her research for practical application Dr. Madlock Gatison is currently serving on the Breast Cancer Consortium Advisory Board. Which is an international partnership committed to the scientific and public discourse about breast cancer, promotes collaborative initiatives among researchers, advocates, health professionals, educators, and others who focus on the systemic factors that impact breast cancer as an individual experience, a social problem, and a health epidemic. She is also a 2013 graduate of the National Breast Cancer Coalitions (NBCC) Project L. E.A. D. institute which is an intensive six day science program taught by renowned research faculty covering the basics of cancer biology, genetics, epidemiology, research design and advocacy. This course and many others that she has attended provide a foundation of scientific knowledge that informs her research and writing.

Dr. Madlock Gatison has presented over 30 papers at regional, national, and international professional conferences. She currently has several forthcoming books and articles due for release in 2015 that include the following: *Embracing the Pink Identity: Breast Cancer Culture,*

Faith Talk and the Myth of the Strong Black Women under contract with Lexington Books due out in Fall 2015; Editor of *Communicating Women's Health: Voicing the Voiceless* under contract with Routledge series in Rhetoric due out in Fall of 2015; *The Pink and The Black Experience: Lies that Make Us Suffer in Silence and Cost Us Our Lives*, an article for Women's Studies in Communication, summer 2015; and *Body Politics Strategies for Inclusiveness: A Case Study of the National Breast Cancer Coalition* a chapter in <u>Contexts for the Dark Side of Communication,</u> Peter Lang Publishing.

Additionally, Madlock Gatison has published multiple articles in the following: *The Sage Deaf Studies Encyclopedia,* 2015; *Encyclopedia of Cancer and Society 2ⁿᵈ Ed,* 2015*; Encyclopedia of Health Communication,* 2014*; Encyclopedia of Multicultural America,* 2013; *Multimedia Encyclopedia of Women in Today's World,* 2012; all with Sage Publishers.

Contact Information:
The Pink and The Black Project
P.O. Box 6162
Hamden, CT 06517

pinkandblackproject@gmail.com

www.ingramcontent.com/pod-product-compliance
Lightning Source LLC
Chambersburg PA
CBHW060157070426
42447CB00033B/2186